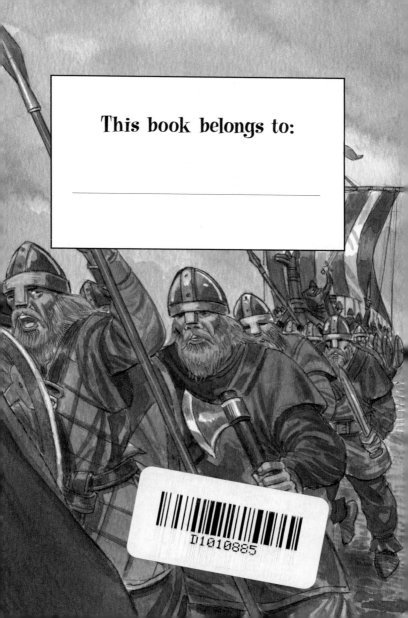

This book belongs to:

_____

Published by Ladybird Books Ltd
A Penguin Company
Penguin Books Ltd, 80 Strand, London WC2R 0RL, UK
Penguin Books Australia Ltd, Camberwell, Victoria, Australia
Penguin Books (NZ) Ltd, Cnr Airbourne and Rosedale Roads, Albany, Auckland, 1310, New Zealand

1 3 5 7 9 10 8 6 4 2

© LADYBIRD BOOKS MMV

Printed in Italy

Vikings

written by Jillian Powell
illustrated by Jim Eldridge

Ladybird

The Vikings lived in northern Europe many years ago.

They were warriors, sailors and farmers.

780–1100 AD
Where the Vikings lived

6

The Vikings lived in houses
like this.

grass roof

thick walls

8

smoke hole

9

The Vikings wore clothes like this.

brooch

over dress

10

wool
cloak

leather
shoes

11

The Vikings ate food
like this.

wild
berries

bread

cabbage

12

meat stew

peas

13

The Vikings played games
like this.

board

playing
pieces

bone
flute

15

The Vikings made tools
like this.

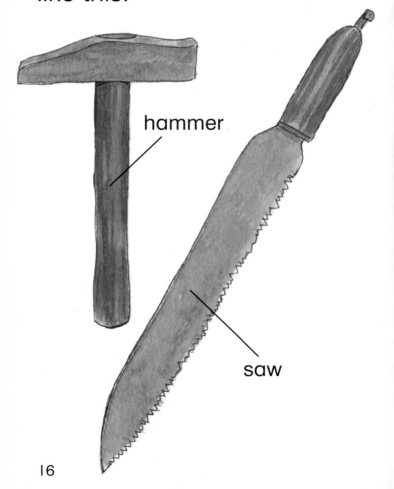

hammer

saw

The Vikings made jewellery like this.

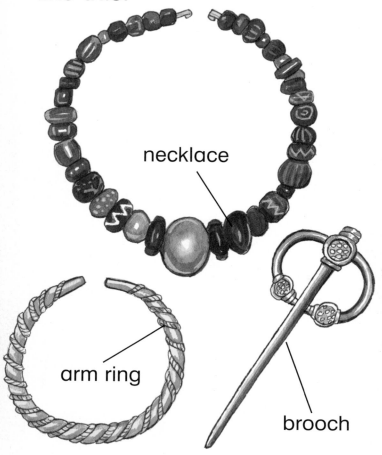

necklace

arm ring

brooch

The Viking women did jobs
like this.

milking
cow

weaving

cooking

21

The Viking men did jobs
like this.

farming

carrying wood

digging

23

The Vikings sailed in ships like this.

dragon head

oar

24

sail

The Vikings fought in battles like this.

helmet

sword

shield

27

What would you do if you were a Viking?

fight

play

sail

weave

farm

29

Index